BLUE LAGOONS AND BEACHES
Fiji's Yasawa Islands

First published 1985 by Millwood Press Ltd.,
291b Tinakori Road, Thorndon, Wellington.
© 1985 James Siers
No part of this book may be reproduced in any manner
whatsoever without the written authority of the
publisher and author.

ISBN 0-908582-76-5

Printed in Singapore

BLUE LAGOONS AND BEACHES

FIJI'S YASAWA ISLANDS

JAMES SIERS

MILLWOOD PRESS   WELLINGTON   NEW ZEALAND

MILLWOOD

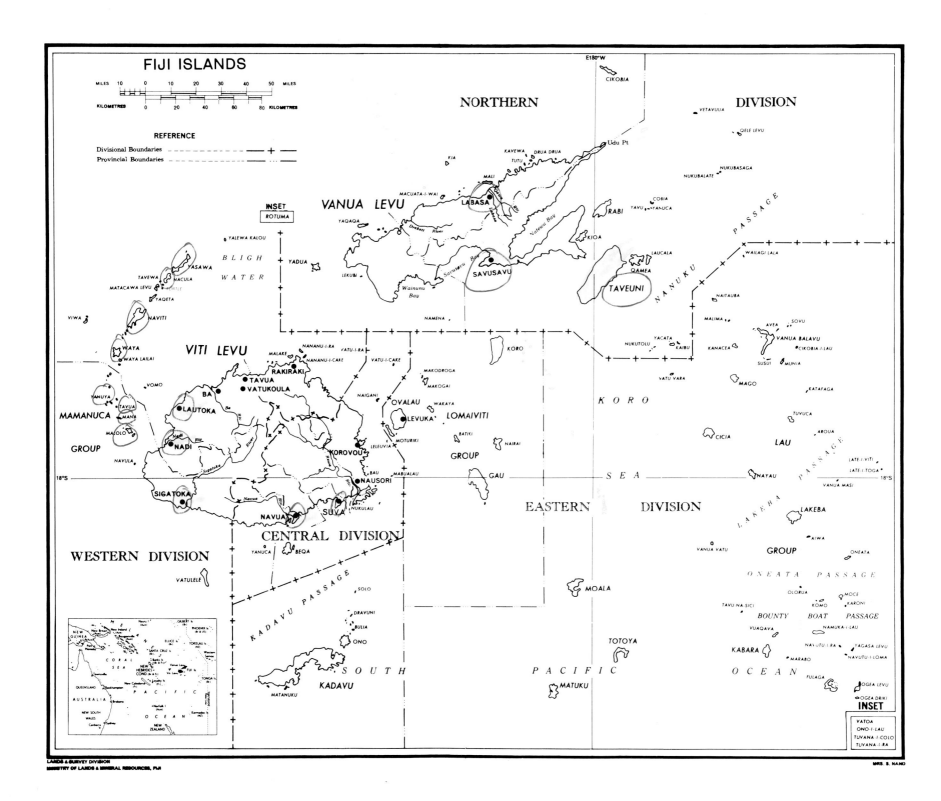

FIJI ISLANDS

MILES 10   0   10   20   30   40   50 MILES

KILOMETRES 0   20   40   60   80 KILOMETRES

REFERENCE

Divisional Boundaries ————— + —————
Provincial Boundaries ————— · —————

INSET
ROTUMA

E180°W

NORTHERN   DIVISION

CIKOBIA

VETAVUUA

QELE LEVU

KAVEWA DRUA DRUA

KIA

TUTU

Udu Pt

MALI

NUKUBASAGA

NUKUBALATE

MACUATA-I-WAI

VANUA LEVU

LABASA

RABI

COBIA

YAVU YANUCA

YAQAQA

KIOA

Dreketi River

LEKUBI

Natewa Bay

LAUCALA

WAILAGI LALA

VANUA LEVU

INSET

YALEWA KALOU

YADUA

BLIGH

WATER

Wainunu Bay

Savusavu Bay

SAVUSAVU

QAMEA

TAVEUNI

NAITAUBA

MALIMA

NAMENA

AVEA SOVU

VANUA BALAVU

CIKOBIA-I-LAU

NANUKU   PASSAGE

YASAWA

TAVEWA NACULA

MATACAWA LEVU

TURTLE

YAQETA

YADUA

NAVITI

NUKUTOLU

YACATA

KAIBU

KANACEA

SUSUI MUNIA

VATU VARA

MAGO

KATAFAGA

VIWA

WAYA

WAYA LAILAI

VITI LEVU

MALAKE

NANANU-I-RA

NANANU-I-CAKE

VATU-I-RA

VATU-I-CAKE

KORO

KORO

TUVUCA

AROUA

RAKIRAKI

TAVUA

VATUKOULA

MAKODROGA

MAKOGAI

NAIGANI

OVALAU

WAKAYA

KORO

SEA

CICIA

LAU

VOMO

BA

LEVUKA

LOMAIVITI

BATIKI

LATE-I-VITI

LATE-I-TOGA

MAMANUCA

YANUYA

TAVUA

MANA

LAUTOKA

Ba River

LELEUVIA

MOTURIKI

NAIRAI

GROUP

NAYAU

VANUA MASI

MALOLO

GROUP

NADI

Nadi River

Rewa River

KOROVOU

GAU

18°S

SEA

18°S

LAKEBA   PASSAGE

LAKEBA

NAVULA

Sigatoka River

BAU

MABUALAU

NAUSORI

EASTERN   DIVISION

AIWA

SIGATOKA

Navua River

Rewa River

SUVA

NUKULAU

AIWA

VANUA VATU

GROUP

ONEATA

WESTERN DIVISION

NAVUA

CENTRAL DIVISION

YANUCA

BEQA

ONEATA   PASSAGE

VATULELE

KADAVU   PASSAGE

SOLO

MOALA

OLORUA

MOCE

KOMO KARONI

TAVU-NA-SICI

VUAQAVA

BOUNTY   BOAT   PASSAGE

NAMUKA-I-LAU

DRAVUNI

BULIA

ONO

TOTOYA

KABARA

NAVUTU-I-RA YAGASA-LEVU

MARABO

NAVUTU-I-LOMA

SOUTH

KADAVU

PACIFIC

OCEAN

FULAGA

OGEA LEVU

MATANUKU

MATUKU

OGEA DRIKI

INSET

INSET
VATOA
ONO-I-LAU
TUVANA-I-COLO
TUVANA-I-RA

THE VERY BEAUTIFUL YASAWA GROUP OF ISLANDS.
MUST BE SEEN TO BE BELEIVED

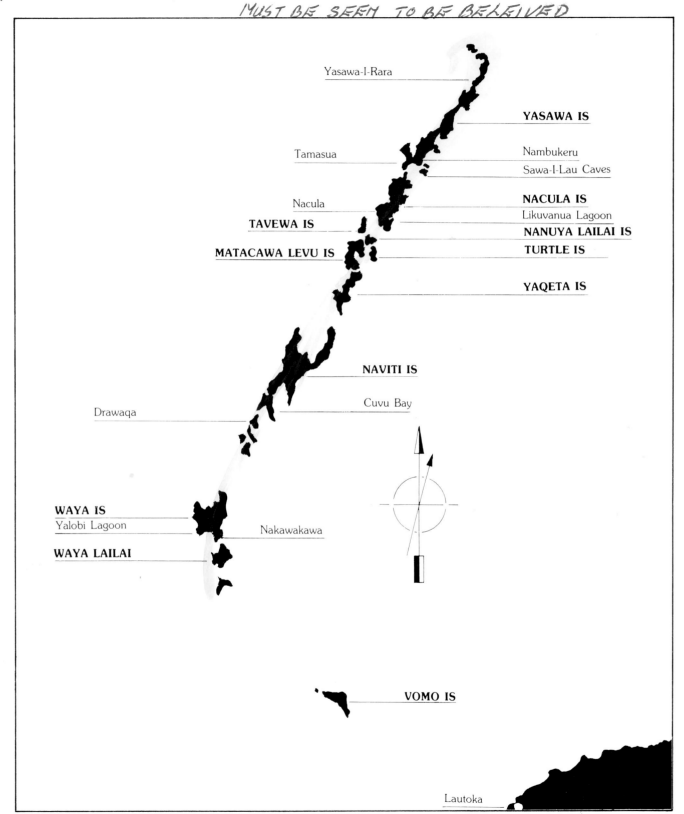

Yasawa-I-Rara

YASAWA IS

Tamasua

Nambukeru

Sawa-I-Lau Caves

Nacula

NACULA IS

Likuvanua Lagoon

TAVEWA IS

NANUYA LAILAI IS

MATACAWA LEVU IS

TURTLE IS

YAQETA IS

NAVITI IS

Cuvu Bay

Drawaqa

WAYA IS

Yalobi Lagoon

Nakawakawa

WAYA LAILAI

VOMO IS

Lautoka

THE BEAUTIFUL AND FRAGRANT PLUMERIA. (FRANGIPANI)

INTRODUCTION

The words "blue lagoon" have become synonymous with a tropical island paradise and in particular with Fiji's fabulous Yasawa Islands. This is not only because of the thousands of people who have enjoyed the Blue Lagoon Cruise through the group, but also because of the two films that were shot in the Yasawas and also titled *The Blue Lagoon*.

The first of these was filmed in 1948. It featured Jean Simmons and Ed Huston and was the first to exploit in colour the exquisite beauty of the islands. The second film starred Brooke Shields and Chris Atkins.

Both films were based on a novel by Henry De Vere Stacpoole and both were shot on Nanuya Levu which is now known as Turtle Island and which lies in the heart of the Yasawa chain.

Stacpoole's novel tells the story of two children who are shipwrecked during the last century while in passage from Sydney to San Francisco. The two children, a boy and a girl, and an old sailor known as Paddy, are the only survivors. They fetch up on an uninhabited tropical island paradise. Paddy cares for the children long enough for them to learn the art of survival so that when he dies, they manage to live very well. The film shows the innocence of their relationship bloom into love. It is a romantic story ideally suited to the unreal beauty of the Yasawa Islands.

The film's title was also the inspiration for Captain Trevor Withers who fell in love with the beauty of the islands and decided to inaugurate a boat cruise which he called the Blue Lagoon. Withers was as much inspired by the courtesy and hospitality of the Yasawa people as he was by the beauty of the islands and took into account that the Fijians called the area near the Sawa i Lau caves, the Blue Lagoon. Withers nearly went bankrupt trying to promote and operate his tourist cruise. This was back in 1950 and in those early years tourism was virtually unknown in Fiji. There were no jet planes which each week now disgorge thousands of visitors. It was only five years since the end of the war. Those who ventured to Fiji most probably considered the effort in getting there sufficient adventure in itself and needed nothing

more. But the few enticed by Trevor Withers to the Yasawa Islands and to his "Blue Lagoon" came back with a missionary zeal. They were converts as many are today to an almost mystical notion that somehow for a few brief inspired moments they had come as close as it was possible to a tourist paradise: This surely was the real thing — unspoiled beauty and unspoiled people, the whole in a resolved peaceful harmony; lovely beaches fringed by tall, nodding coconut palms, the sand dazzling white and so fine that in some places the Fijians call it seven-day sand because it takes seven days to wash it out if you get it in your hair. In those days only a few people lived in the Yasawas so that there was a feeling of cruising in a lovely wilderness with an occasional village tucked away among the greenery.

Trevor Withers continued to struggle for several years, always on the verge of bankruptcy but always managing to survive, until finally sufficient passengers were on hand for the enterprise to prosper. A more detailed account of the Blue Lagoon Cruise will be found in the pages that follow.

In the past fifteen years some 20,000 people have visited the Yasawa Islands each year on the Blue Lagoon Cruise. Others have come to stay at the exclusive Turtle Island Lodge. Most of them have asked questions about the islands and about the culture of the people who live there. This book attempts in words and pictures to answer most of such questions.

The system of orthography used in this text was devised in the last century by English missionaries. It is the official system and for those who do not understand its structure, highly confusing. The township of Nadi is pronounced Nandi; Sigatoka is Singatoka; the island of Nacula where your cruise boat will stop, is pronounced Nathula; Nabukeru village near the Sawa i Lau caves, is Nambukeru.

The rules are:
All vowels are sounded as on the Continent:
"A" is long as in answer
"E" is long as in pet
"I" is pronounced as in bee and thus, Viti Levu is (Veetee Levoo)
"O" is long as in order
"U" is long as in Lucy
Unusual Fijian consonant sounds are accounted for thus:
"B" is always MB as in remember
"D" is always ND as in candy
"Q" is a G as in great
"C" is Th as in them
"G" is soft as in singalong.

The following list of English and Fijian words and their pronunciation will prove helpful to those who are interested:

ENGLISH	FIJIAN	PRONOUNCED
GOOD MORNING	NI SA YADRA	*nee sar yarndra*
GREETINGS/HELLO/HI	NI SA BULA	*nee sa bula*
GOOD BYE	SA MOCE	*sar more there*
PLEASE	YALO VINAKA	*yarlo vee narka*
EXCUSE ME	TULOU	*too low*
YES	IO	*eee or*
THANK YOU/GOOD	VINAKA	*vee narka*
THANK YOU VERY MUCH	VINAKA VAKA LEVU	*vee narka varkar levoo*
MUCH OR BIG	LEVU	*levoo*
NO	SEGA	*senga*
EAT	KANA	*kar na*
VILLAGE	KORO	*ko ro*
LADY/MADAM	MARAMA	*marama*
MR/SIR	TURAGA	*tu ra nga*
A LITTLE/SMALL	VAKA LAILAI	*va ka lie lie*
GREAT/A LOT	VAKA LEVU	*va ka le vu*
FAST	VAKA TOTOLO	vaka tortorlo
HOUSE	VALE	*va le*
TOILET	VALE LAILAI	*va le lie lie*
COME	LAKO MAI	*la ko my*
GO	LAKO TANI	*la ko tan i*
BRING	KAUTA MAI	*kow ta my*
TAKE AWAY	KAUTA TANI	*la ko tan i*
ONE MORE	DUA TALE	*dua a ta le*
ONE	DUA	*du a*
TWO	RUA	*ru a*
WHAT IS THIS	NA CAVA OQO	*na thava ornggor*
SLOWLY	VAKA MALUA	*va ka mar lua*

The Yasawa Islands lie in a spectacular chain to the northwest of Viti Levu. There are six principal islands and approximately sixty smaller islands, islets and sand cays. Except for those employed at Turtle Island or the descendents of the Irishman William Doughty who live on Tavewa Island, the population of 4000 people is Fijian. The people live traditionally in villages, surrounded by their kin and sharing customary land. They pay homage to hereditary chiefs and observe the many cultural traditions which are so much part of the Fijian way of life. This way of life depends to a large extent on a cooperative approach to major tasks such as the building of houses; the construction of churches (and the fundraising to make this possible); certain types of planting and fishing and general help to those with blood ties however remote these may be.

A Yasawa Islander is born into a cocoon of collective security. Should anything happen to his mother and father, the child will be cared for by any of a number of kin eager to have him. These may be grandparents, uncles and aunties (who are in fact known in Fijian terms as mothers and fathers) or the first cousins of the parents, whom the Fijians recognise as brothers and sisters. The children grow up with rights to the use of land from which they obtain food crops, house-building material, and cash crops such as copra. They also have rights to the reefs and sea which are recognised as belonging to the group.

As the child grows in a typical Yasawa community he or she will be brought up to respect their parents and elders and to put community interests ahead of their own. In return for supporting the group, the group will support them.

There are primary and secondary schools in the Yasawa Islands. The new generation is bi-lingual and much more aware of the world beyond its immediate shores. Brighter children go to the mainland to high school and then to University at Suva. Too often they come back and sink without trace into the peace of subsistance farming, fishing and village life. In that sense, life is far too easy. Some who have chosen to return and settle back among their communities are torn between two worlds. On the one hand they crave the material goods and the personal freedome they see enjoyed by their Indian, European, Chinese and part-European contemporaries, but most of them abhor the competitive effort needed to achieve those goods and goals. It is also completely against their nature to want to cut themselves off from their friends and relatives and invariably those who do, look upon their absence as temporary.

The Fijian community functions on sharing. *Kerekere* is a word that has its counterpart throughout the South Pacific. Specifically it is a request that cannot be denied. Within a kinship group property is deemed communal and it is not unusual to see the same item of clothing worn by different people on different days. A gift acquired from a relative on the mainland or from a visitor will also quickly make the rounds.

There are some things which while they may be borrowed are also clearly recognised as belonging to someone. Boats, spearguns, engines and such fall into this category. Whilst an individual may gain stature through the possession of such items, he also has to care for them whilst those who use them do not. In this light the custom of *kerekere* is a disincentive. It assures the individual of support and it must be most comforting to know you can descent on your uncles, aunties or cousins — even distant ones — with perfect assurance that they will share with you everything they have got. Unfortunately, especially away from the Yasawa Islands, there is often little to share but even so, it is never shared grudgingly as it would be in a comparable situation in the United States, Australia or New Zealand. Because each Fijian knows he must share he also knows that his enterprise and initiative will work to the benefit of others. There is little point in producing a surplus. The *kerekere* system also works in making sure that goods are shared and that individuals with energy and initiative do not rise above others except only in specific, clearly defined areas. It is always in projects which are seen to benefit the community, such as in the building of churches, schools and dispensaries that work is contributed ungrudgingly. This is also true of house-building, especially when it comes to the construction of traditional *bures,* where custom is most specific about the help to be contributed.

A Yasawa Fijian will say: "I have my land, my house, the sea and reefs, my family and my friends. What else do I need?"

His view may be shared by many who live in the Lau Islands, Kadavu, Beqa, Lomaiviti or Vatulele, where traditions still govern day to day activities. But I suspect those Fijians are like everyone else and that they want more: better schooling for their children; better housing; better medical facilities; better communications; jobs which pay well and have status and I wonder how they can get them.

The Yasawa people are fortunate. They welcomed Trevor Withers to their shores to begin an association which has brought benefits to their islands and opened possibilities for the future which will meet many of their aspirations. The Blue Lagoon Cruises provide jobs; pay fees for access rights; for entertainment; and they bring visitors to villages to purchase shells and handicrafts. Turtle Island Lodge also provides jobs and with it training in important skills such as construction, electrical wiring, sewage reticulation, water conservation and by making the people aware of opportunities which lie on their doorstep.

Trevor Withers died in 1981 and by request, his ashes were scattered over the waters surrounding the islands he had come to love so much. Before he died, he had the satisfaction in knowing that his vision had been realised. The company he started with all his meager earthly possessions is now a large multi-million dollar corporation whose continuing success is a guarantee to the

Yasawa people of greater benefits.

In appreciation of the friendship and assistance of the Yasawa people, Trevor Withers established several dispensary-clinics near the larger schools in the group. He provided sporting equipment and scholarships for the secondary education of deserving children. Since 1966 Blue Lagoon Cruises has greatly increased the provision of financial and educational facilities. It helped with the construction of schools in Yalobi, Nacula and Nabukeru. It has paid school fees, supplied books and uniforms for children in and from the group. Islanders also receive dividends from a parcel of stock units in the company presented to them as a gesture of thanks.

PRE-HISTORY

The Fiji Islands are recognised as the cultural cauldron of the central Pacific region. It was here that the Negrito Melanesians met with a Malay-type people and over an intervening millenia developed a distinct racial type and for the most part adopted what we recognise today as a Polynesian culture. The first settlement of Fiji occurred possibly as early as 2000 B.C. Traces of the settlements of these early arrivals have been uncovered and dated to pre-1500 B.C. Archaeologists credit the first arrival in Fiji to the ancestors of the Polynesians whom they have called the "Lapita" people. "Lapita" is a term applied to pottery first discovered in New Caledonia and named after the site where it was found. It has since been found in a trail that leads from New Ireland and New Britain in Papua New Guinea to the Solomon Islands, Vanuatu, New Caledonia, Tonga, Samoa and the Marquesas Islands to the north-east of Tahiti. The most interesting aspect of the pottery shards found in the Marquesas Islands is the fact that the pots were made in Fiji from material found in the Rewa River delta near Suva. For many centuries Fijian pottery was one of the trade items with Tonga and Samoa and it is possible that a canoe from one of these island groups carried pots to the Marquesas Islands, possibly on the initial voyage of discovery and settlement.

Whoever the Lapita people were is not known, and after their sojourn in Fiji, where they had more than a thousand years of interaction with Melanesian people, the original racial composition of those intrepid voyagers and bold discoverers will never be known. The two groups had a profound effect on each other. The small-statured Melanesians benefitted from an admixture of "Lapita" blood to the extent that Fijians are among some of the tallest people in the Pacific basin. Despite the inter-

action it would seem that the two groups kept apart and that eventually the "Lapita" people now considerably modified with Melanesian blood and culture were forced out into the Lau islands and then to the Tongan archipelago. From Tonga it is a short step to Samoa, Niue, the Cook Islands and Tahiti. Tahiti and the Marquesas Islands would appear to have been the launching points of many voyages of discovery so that by the time of the Battle of Hastings when William the Conqueror took England all the islands of the vast Pacific had been discovered and settled. These included such distant places as Hawaii, Easter Island and New Zealand.

Knowledge of Fiji was retained by succeeding generations. In Tahiti a navigator drew a map for the famous English discoverer, Captain James Cook. The Tahitian drew the map on sand with pebbles indicating the various island groups known to him. This included Fiji. It seems highly probable that Tahiti is in fact named after Fiji which in the Tahitian dialect would be known as Hiti. The Fijian language is part of the same language used by Polynesians and for those who know it, the similarity with Tongan, Samoan and east Polynesian dialects is readily apparent. In Samoa, for example, Fiji would be known as Fiti and in New Zealand as Whiti.

Students of history can speculate on the early years of the settlement of Fiji. It is easy to imagine how vast the land must have seemed to a boat of weary voyagers and with what apprehension they must have approached it. We can also imagine their relief and delight when they found themselves to be the sole proprietors of such a vast inheritance. Imagine also the abundance of resources.

At first there was a limitless choice of where to settle and where to plant the food crops which the voyagers brought with them; taro, breadfruit, papaya, bananas, sugarcane, yams and the other useful crops such as the paper mulberry from which to make bark cloth. It may be that they also brought the coconut. They also brought with them the pig, the dog and the jungle cock and probably also the rat. The settlers continued making pottery and maintained their ability to build and sail canoes.

At some stage after the initial settlement human bones began to appear in oven middens. It is obvious that human flesh had been cooked and that it was eaten along with the flesh of birds, fish, dogs and rats. As cannabalism was also practiced by Polynesians, it is difficult to know who introduced it. The Fijians say the practice was begun by the people of Gau Island not far from Suva. By the time of European contact in the early 1800s, war and cannibalism were endemic and practiced in such a relentless way that it was a wonder there were any people left in Fiji.

At the time of European contact knowledge of the first discovery had passed from race memory. Fijians for the most part attribute their origin to the chiefs Lutonasobasoba and Degei who arrived from the west in their great double canoe, the *Kaunitoni*. The canoe passed through the Yasawa Islands where the voyagers camped for some time; continued through the Mamanuca group and eventually made landfall at Vuda near the present village of Viseisei. Degei and some of his followers trekked round the northern coast, past what is now Lautoka, Ba, Tavua and Rakiraki where they ascended the Kauvadra mountains and established a settlement on the slopes. Degei's descendents came to dominate Eastern Fiji, founding chiefdoms now regarded as the antecedents of most of Fiji's principal families. The legend of Lutonasobasoba clearly acknowledges that they were not the first people in Fiji. Degei's progeny took women to wife from the people they found already occupying the land. It is generally accepted that 500 years is the maximum period for an oral history to be retained with some degree of accuracy. On that basis, Lutunasobasoba and Degei were clearly recent arrivals. It is reasonable to suppose that they were probably Polynesians and most likely Tongans. The Melanesians to this day do not have high chiefs nor a history of having had them in the way that the Polynesians do.

It is not possible to say how the Yasawa Islands featured in the discovery of Fiji, but it is reasonable to assume they may have been the first sighted by voyagers from the west. The island of Naviti (it is Viti: Fiji) suggests that it was the first touched by the discoverers and named by them before they continued their voyage to the mainland which they called Viti Levu (great Viti).

At the time of European contact the Yasawa Islands were held by a number of contending chiefs. They acknowledged no controlling authority. Their people were almost constantly at war with the other island peoples and with succeeding waves of invaders from the mainland.

The people of Naviti trace their descent from a group which came from Lautoka several generations ago and conquered the island. The people of Nacula Island trace their descent from an invading party near Ba. In some cases, as on the island of Yasawa, the invaders were not strong enough to take the whole island but managed to secure a part of it. In the mid 1800s, the Tongan chief, Maafu, came through the group and imposed for the time being his power over the islands by right of conquest. Maafu lost his *mana* when Fiji became a British Crown colony in 1874 and the Yasawa Islands, now largely Christian and at peace between themselves and the rest of Fiji, could quietly become forgotten. In that period only two islands were alienated. These were Tavewa and Nanuya Levu. Part of Nanuya Lailai was also sold but the rest of the group remains in Fijian ownership.

ISA LEI

Isa, Isa, vulagi lasa dina
Nomu lako, au na rarawa kina
Cava beka, ko a mai cakava
Nomu lako, au na sega ni lasa.

Chorus:
Isa lei, na noqu rarawa
Ni ko sa na vodo e na mataka
Bau nanuma, na nodatou lasa
Mai Nanuya nanuma tikoga.

Vanua rogo, na nomuni vanua
Kena ca, ni levu tu na ua
Lomaqu voli, meu bau butuka
Tovolea, ke balavu na bula.

Domoni dina, na nomu yanuyanu
Kena kau, wale na salusalu
Moce lolo, bua, na kukuwalu
Lagakali, bab no rosidamu.

ISA LEI

Isa, isa, you are my only treasure
Must you leave me, so lonely and forsaken
As the roses will miss the sun at dawning
Every moment my heart for you is yearning.

Chorus:
Isa lei, the purple shadows fall
Sad the morrow will dawn upon my sorrow
Oh! Forget not, when you are far away
Precious moments beside Nanuya Bay.

Isa, Isa, my heart was filled with pleasure
From the moment I heard your tender greeting
Mid the sunshine, we spent the hours together
Now so swifly those happy hours are fleeting.

O'er the ocean your island home is calling
Happy country where roses bloom in splendour
Oh! If I could but journey there beside you
Then forever my heart would sing in rapture.

The Yasawa Islands enjoy a warm dry climate with little rainfall. While this is greatly appreciated by visitors, it is not appreciated by villagers who often suffer droughts. Many of the islands have built reservoirs and catchments near springs so that water is available in villages from taps. It is a luxury much enjoyed by the children.

These pictures were taken at the village of Somosomo which lies in a spectacular bay at the northern end of the island of Naviti. The island is the biggest in the group and has six villages, including the large settlement at Soso.

13

These aerial views show details of Naviti. Above lie the villages of Naviti and Malevu. The primary and intermediate school draws pupils from nearby islands as well as the villages of Naviti. The children from Somosomo spend approximately two hours each day walking to school over the mountain ridge which lies to the right of the school. The most striking feature, to my mind, is the colour of the coral heads in the bay.

Right: the line of islands on the north-east tip of Naviti offers this spectacular aerial view. There is a small boat harbour, often used by visiting yachts, between the fourth and fifth islands and the colour of the water clearly indicates the entrance to the anchorage. It is here also that the remains of an American fighter aeroplane lie in shallow water. The pilot, who was returning from a reconnaisance flight to the north, ran out of fuel approximately 16 kilometres away, just over the southern tip of Yasawa Island. He was able to glide to Naviti where he put the plane down in the calm lagoon behind the row of islands and lived to tell the tale.

The island of Yasawa, which is the northern-most of the group, is seen in these two views with the village of Bukama as a reference point. The view above is to the north whilst the plate opposite shows the island stretching away to the south. Yasawa island is the longest in the group. Both views were taken from the eastern side. The village of Bukama is one of the most traditional in the group. Only the school, the church and two other buildings are not *bures*.

The village was originally sited in a strong defensive fort on the headland. Legend says it fell to an invading force from somewhere near Ba. The victors took the spoils, but these also included a running fued with the people of Yasawa-i-Rara to the north and the people of Teci to the south.

Bukama was one of the most pleasant villages I visited during the course of the photographic assignment and this may be because it is so completely off the beaten track and the people seldom have visitors. We arrived at sunset, having come around the northern tip of Yasawa Island in a 5-metre dinghy. The scene made an unforgettable impression. The village is guarded on each side by imposing bluffs and on the southern bluff, goats were outlined against the sunet. Beyond the beach there was a line of tall coconut trees and under these a row of thatched *bures*. Our guide, Ratu Joe, from Matacawalevu Village, was almost instantly discovered by one of his cousins and we were whisked away to be looked after for the night.

From the island of Yaqeta looking north. Yaqeta lies just south of the centre of the group. It is possible to discern the high peak of Sawa i Lau at the southern tip of Yasawa Island. It is here that the famous caves may be found. *Opposite,* the view shows the passage between the islands of Yaqeta and Matacawalevu.

It is impossible sometimes to believe the colours of the lagoon around the Yasawas. I always come away with the impression that a wonderful artist devised a complimentary scheme of blues, greens, turquoise and at certain times tans and purple. I spent approximately two hours in a small aeroplane flying around the islands. The overall impression was breathtaking.

These views are a study of colour. *Above,* one of the many lagoons on the western side of Naviti is truly a classic "blue lagoon". There are literally hundreds like this along the length of the island chain.

Opposite, a lagoon a little to the south of the village of Yasawa i Rara. The village is sighted at the northern tip of Yasawa Island. There is a good deal of debate as to where in the Yasawa Islands the real "blue lagoon" may be found. I believe it is found anywhere you want to find it, on either east or west coast of any of the islands from Waya to Yasawa. As in love, it is a question of preference.

ALL OF THE ISLANDS OF THE YASAWA GROUP ARE TRULY BEAUTIFUL AND THE COLOURS ARE EVEN MORE MAGNIFICENT THAN YOU SEE THEM HERE IN PRINT. WHEN YOU FLY OVER THE ISLANDS BY SEAPLANE OR THE TINY "TURTLE ISLAND" AIRLINES, THE ISLANDS LOOK LIKE A NECKLACE OF OPALS IN AN UNBELIEVABLE BLUE SEA.

The eastern coast of the Yasawa Islands is like a giant saw with great teeth of coral forever cutting into the sea. Or it may be that the ocean is like a giant battering ram, which when propelled by eastern trade winds, has broken its way past the island's defensive breastworks and cut deep channels to the very edge of the land. Such deep channels are welcomed by the islanders as they form protected harbours for their small craft. *Above*, the village of Vuaki on the island of Matacawalevu is recognised as a sheltered anchorage in times of cyclones. *Opposite*, the island of Nacula.

22

The title of this book is *Blue Lagoons and Beaches* and it is most appropriate. I have tried to estimate — for my own satisfaction — the number of beaches to be found throughout the Yasawa Islands and found it impossible. I know there are hundreds and that each one is better than any of a number of famous beaches, such as for example Waikiki at Honolulu, Hawaii. How do you measure such quality? By the texture of the sand and the warmth, purity and clarity of its water? By such standards the Yasawa beaches are outstanding.

Above, a view of the beach at Nacula Island at its south-western tip and *left*, the beach at Soso, Naviti Island.

WE HAVE WALKED ALL THESE BEAUTIFUL WHITE BEACHES, AND FOUND TREASURES OF SHELLS. ROGER AND I HAVE DONE THESE ISLANDS 5 TIMES WITH 3 CRUISES ON THE "YASAWA PRINCESS"

The people who dwell in the Yasawa Islands seldom contemplate the beauty of their beaches. Their attitude is shaped by survival and the constant daily struggle with the land and the sea from which they obtain their food, their building materials and their cash crops. In the past they also obtained their clothes, canoes, sails and rope from what the soil and bush offered. The beach has always been the place from which you either go into the sea or from which you launch your boat. You will never find islanders sunbathing as we do. Children will play on beaches and in the water but their parents will only go into it to bathe or to seek food. Thus, the man I photographed in his *kasava* patch on the island of Matacawalevu was more concerned with how much yield his plants would give than with the beautiful beach below him. *Right,* the children of Nabukeru, who picked up shells for this photograph, were equally puzzled that in my view, the scene was remarkable. The Fijians do not lack appreciation of beauty. Chief's *bures*, sailing canoes of former times, weapons, fans, fine mats, baskets and personal ornaments, were works of art.

The photograph is a variation of the scene chosen for the dust jacket of this book and is a view from Nabukeru Village towards the island of Sawa i Lau. A Blue Lagoon Cruise boat is anchored near the island.

A sand cay snakes its way out to a rock outcrop on the island of Naviti. The sail of a visiting yacht can be seen in the blue water beyond the reef. *Right*, this view is from Tavewa Island looking towards Nanuya Lailai in the centre of the Yasawa group.

Morning and evening, especially during the "summer" season between November and March, is the time for spectacular sunrises and sunsets. The view above is from Turtle Island looking towards Matacawalevu and Tavewa. *Opposite,* the high peak of Sawa i Lau is the landmark to identify this scene. The picture was taken from the northern shore of Nacula Island.

The people of the Yasawa Islands live in villages in traditional clan groupings. Many things have changed in the past thirty years. The view above is of Matacawalevu Village and shows a preponderance of iron roofs and concrete block houses in contrast to the lines of *bures* which comprise the village of Teci (opposite page).

Matacawalevu has benefitted from employment opportunities on Blue Lagoon cruise boats; jobs with the Turtle Island Lodge and through work as extras in the filming of the movie, *The Blue Lagoon*. The village is strategically placed to take advantage of employment opportunities in contrast to the community at Teci which is on the eastern coast of Yasawa Island and therefore out of reach of cruise boats and jobs. To this day villages are set out in a neat plan around a central open area where at one end, usually on a raised mound, the chief's bure is sited.

There is no doubt that whilst visitors prefer to see people living in traditional *bures*, the people prefer to live in block houses. There is something to be said for both. The *bure* may be built quickly and without cost, except for incidentals such as food for the builders. It is well insulated and for that reason is always cool in the heat of summer. Its disadvantage is its limited lifespan. Block houses are usually bigger and when completed require little maintenance. They also confer status on their owners. Recently there has been a resurgence of *bure* construction due to a recession of the economy and the return of people from the mainland.

Last year, the villagers of Namara at Waya Sewa awoke in the night to the roar of an avalanche which threatened to demolish their village. Thousands of tonnes of earth and rock came down the hillside but miraculously no house was touched and no one was injured. The villagers took their escape as a warning and have abandoned their old site. *Topright*, four schoolchildren from the village of Malakaite were not so lucky. As they were on their way to school at Nacula one morning, the rocks peeled off the cliff face and buried them. The site is pointed to visitors as the scene of one of the worst disasters in the Yasawas since the end of the tribal wars. *Right*, the coming of Christianity helped to promote peace in the group and this year (1985) the centenary of the founding of the Wesleyan Mission in the Yasawas was celebrated. At Naisisili village on the island of Nacula it was marked with a commemorative stone outside the chief's *bure*.

One of the marvels in the Yasawa Islands is the church at Soso, Naviti, which was completed in 1979 at a cost of $23,000 for the materials only. All the labour was contributed free of charge by the villagers. The church is the result of a collaboration of the chief, Ratu Vuki Beloloa and the builder, Joseva Waibune, from eastern Fiji.

Joseva, featured (left), designed the church, supervised its construction and interior outfitting and then painstakingly carved the decorations himself. *Above*, a view of the church from the rear door. *Top left,* the alter, pulpit and lectern.

The church at Soso is the grandest in the Yasawas and somewhat out of keeping with the Wesleyan abhorrence of ostentation, but much in keeping with Fijian devotion. The church at Nacula village, *above,* is more in style of what may be seen in the islands. *Extreme left,* Ratu Vuki Beloloa stands beside the historic stone at Soso. It was brought to Naviti more than 100 years ago by the people of Soso, Kadavu Island. A similar stone went back to Kadavu, to mark the special relationship between the two villages on account of a marriage of a Kadavu woman to the chief of Soso, Naviti. *Left,* in some cases Fijians bury their dead inside the village, often putting up elaborate tombs and headstones.

Visitors to the Yasawa Islands tend to see their new world in a romantic light. A housewife emerging from Sydney's suburban neurosis would view a scene such as the one above as idyllic. But whilst most Fijians would readily change places with her, I am certain that most women from Sydney or Auckland or Los Angeles would not. This is not to say that European women would not adapt, but given the choice they would rather not try.

Fijians have welcomed visitors to their shores because they see tourism as an important industry which filters down to the village level where the sale of shells, artefacts and curiosities can be a source of cash. Yasawa Islanders will often say: We are rich in land, in the sea and in our reefs but poor in not having money.

Right, a Government supply ship off Naviti.

The sale of shells, necklaces, handicrafts and curiosities is an important source of cash in the Yasawa Islands — a fact made obvious by comparing villages which are on the tourist route and those which are not.

45

Captain Trevor Withers, seen here in the company of the former Governor-General of Fiji, Ratu Sir George Cabokabu, was the visionary who began the Blue Lagoon cruise 35 years ago in 1950. He came to Fiji not long after the end of the Second World War with his friend, the renowned Australian aviator, Harold Gatty. They were looking at the possibility of establishing a fishing industry. Gatty had won fame for his "around the world in 80 days" flight with American co-pilot, Wiley Post. Withers had also been involved in aviation, having planned the setting up of trunk services between major New Zealand cities.

Withers and Gatty spent four years conducting a feasibility study into the practicality of setting up the fishing industry with particular reference to the large schools of tuna which were known to abound in Fijian waters. At the end of this period, they decided the project was not viable and wound up the venture. Both, however, decided they wanted to stay in Fiji. Gatty went on to establish Fiji Airways, the forerunner of Air Pacific and Trevor Withers decided he would try a tourist cruise through the Yasawa Islands which had made an unforgettable impression upon him.

In 1948 Withers assisted in the making of the film, *The Blue Lagoon*, which was shot in the Yasawa Islands and he chose the name as an appropriate one for the cruise he was planning.

A critical role in the final success of the cruise was played by the people of Yalobi Village on the island of Waya. Withers was to establish a lasting friendship with the senior chief, Tui Waya, and a young villager, Epeli Voli, who became a crew member and an interpreter. The people of the Yasawa Islands gave Withers their unanimous approval to bring tourists to their shores. His friend, Harold Gatty was

not as enthusiastic.

"Where are the tourists?" he asked.

The answer to that question was: there were none.

Withers struggled for ten years to establish his Blue Lagoon cruise, in the process selling all his worldly possessions to keep the operation going.

Question: What do you do if there are no tourists? Answer: You go and get them and this is what Trevor Withers did. He went to the United States and during the course of five weeks hosted 31 cocktail parties. While this promotional effort was to pay long-term dividends, in the short term it was still disasterous for Withers had spent the last of his cash reserves and the tourists were still not coming.

A local copra planter saved the venture from imminent bankruptcy. The injection of fresh capital allowed Withers to keep operating until the effect of his American tour began to pay. At last the tourists came and to such an extent that a new boat was commissioned.

In 1966 — 26 years from the inauguration of the cruise — Trevor Withers sold his company to a fellow New Zealand, Captain Claude Millar. The sale was prompted by ill health which unfortunately Captain Withers had begun to suffer.

Claude Millar formed a new company which he registered as Blue Lagoon Cruises Limited. He soon had two Fairmile launches in service but in taking a long term view, he could see that a new vessel, specially designed for the Yasawa Island conditions was required and took the bold step to commission the Government Shipyard in Suva to build the 39 metre *Lycianda*. The ship was launched in 1970 and became a prototype for what has finally become a modern fleet.

In 1978 Claude Millar retired and returned to New Zealand, selling his interest to Marine Management Ltd, which took a controlling interest in Blue Lagoon Cruises under the direction of its chairman, David Wilson. The company immediately upgraded the operation and as Claude Millar had done in his time, took a long-term view. The result of that view was another milestone: the placement of an order with the Government Shipyard for the biggest and most luxurious ship to be built in Fiji — the 1000 tonne *Yasawa Princess*. The *Yasawa Princess* entered service this year on a seven-day cruise, complementing the existing three-day cruise and I was fortunate to be invited on the inaugural cruise and to witness many of the ceremonies performed in honour of the ship and its complement of VIP guests.

Trevor Withers died in 1981, but had he lived to see the *Yasawa Princess* he would not have been surprised by its magnificence: he knew that one day the islands would win their deserved reputation and with the *Yasawa Princess* a vessel appropriate to their grandeur.

The *Yasawa Princess* at anchor off Yalobi Village, Waya Island.

Left, the 300-metre peak of Sawa i Lau Island off the south-eastern tip of Yasawa Island. Nabukeru Village is to the right and two Blue Lagoon Cruises liners are in the bay. The Island of Sawa i Lau is a coral upthrust honeycombed with caves. The islands are principally of basalt structure having been torn away from south eastern Viti Levu and either twisted away to their present position or Viti Levu has been turned on its axis. Fiji was once part of a large mass which included New Caledonia and Tonga. The islands are still drifting apart at the rate of approximately two centimetres a year.

WE ANCHORED & STAYED HERE 2 DAYS. WE HAD BARB-B QUES ON THE BEACH AND DANCING BY TORCH LIGHT.

Left, the *Yasawa Princess* at anchor off Nanuya Lailai in one of the most magnificent anchorages to be found in the Fiji group. The anchorage lies to the leeward of the prevailing trade wind and is steep-to so that cruise boats can tie up to the coconut trees on the shore. The beach is typical fine, white sand as may be found throughout the Yasawas, with a large area clear of coral for comfortable bathing. In the foreground may be seen a coral reef.

Right, a wide view of Somosomo Bay, Naviti Island. A series of beaches sweep away as far as the eye can see.

A feature of the Yasawa Islands is the number of anchorages which offer shelter regardless of the direction of the wind.

A Blue Lagoon cruise is a series of new destinations where guests are ferried ashore for visits to villages, for sunbathing and swimming from white-sand beaches, barbeque lunches, snorkelling trips and evenings under starlit skies with the aroma of freshly cooked food as it is taken out of the *lovo* (earth oven). Afterwards there is dancing to live music from the ship's crew either on deck or barefoot on the sand.

SO MANY BEAUTIFUL EVENINGS SPENT DANCING FIJI STYLE AT THE BACK OF THE SHIP, DRINKING KAVA. ALL THE CREW JOIN IN THE FUN.

LOVO AT MANUYA LAILAI   LOOK AT ALL THAT DELICIOUS ISLAND FOOD.

Above, the *Yasawa Princess* seen at Nanuya Lailai from another angle. The beach and sandspit are clearly defined by the "blue lagoon". The island of Mata-cawalevu is seen at the top left corner in this view as is part of the village. Fifty acres of the Nanuya Lailai have been purchased by Blue Lagoon Cruises from Burns Philp South Seas. It was part of a copra plantation and the coconut trees will remain.

Right, a view from the north. It shows part of Nanuya Lailai with the cruise boat near the beach; beyond on the left is a tip of Turtle Island and on the right Mata-cawalevu, and in the distance the island of Yaqeta.

The inaugural cruise of the *Yasawa Princess* was the occasion for important traditional Fijian ceremonial. In former times the arrival of a friendly canoe was the opportunity for the hosts to display their wealth and hospitality. One of the more charming ceremonies, being enacted here (in a modified form), was the presentation of fine mats to the warriors fleet-footed enough to catch the women who are seen waving them. The women would wait for the warriors to touch the shore before running to a designated spot. Those taken by the men would become their wives. On this occasion the men had to be content with a share of the mats.

Symbolically, the first village touched in the Yasawas by the *Yasawa Princess* was Yalobi at Waya. This was also the first village touched by Captain Trevor Withers nearly forty years ago when he was conducting his fisheries survey and subsequently by his cruise boat, the *Turaga Levu*. The Tui Waya and his people extended a generous welcome to the Management of Blue Lagoon Cruises and to their VIP guests, which included two Ministers of the Crown, the chiefs of the other islands in the Yasawa group, the Commissioner Western and other important dignitaries. The scenes shown here feature the *yaqona* ceremony.

ON OUR LAST VISIT HERE, MAR/87 ROGER WAS GUEST OF HONOR AT THIS VERY SPECIAL KAVA CEREMONY AND WAS HONOURED BY THE CHIEFS AFTER THE CEREMONY I PASSED AROUND THE REST OF MY CIGARET PACKAGE, IT PLEASED THEM GREATLY. HA. I ALSO GAVE WHATEVER PENS & PENCILS I HAD TO THE CHILDREN. MUST ALWAYS REMEMBER TO TAKE PENS & PENCILS, WRITING PAPER & CIGARETTES AS LITTLE GIFTS — ALSO CUTE PINS. IT DOES NOT TAKE MUCH TO PLEASE THESE BEAUTIFUL PEOPLE.

Left, the ceremony of the presentation of the *tabua* is among one of the most important in Fiji. In former times it was the price of life and death. Nothing could be accomplished without its presentation. The *tabua* is the tooth of the sperm whale and has little value except for its symbolic importance.

Right, the preparation and serving of *yaqona* is equally important. It is a ritual the visitor is more likely to have a chance of witnessing because the Fijians are addicted to its use and will have it when the opportunity offers. On important occasions it is conducted according to strict ritual, each phase, from the setting up of the *yaqona* bowl, to the mixing and straining of the powder performed punctilliously according to local custom until the final moment when the brew is ready to serve. This is generally the critical moment because the master of ceremonies must determine the importance of the guests and the precedence in the service. Even today, a wrong decision as to who may be served first, can cause much ill feeling. In Western Samoa only a few years ago such an incident led to murder.

Yaqona is made from the dried root of the pepper shrub, *piper methysticum.* The root is pounded into a fine powder, mixed with water, strained with hibiscus fibres and then served. A good brew looks like muddy water. It has a unique taste, which some people find refreshing. After quaffing a *bilo* (coconut half shell) of the mixture a general numbing of the throat is usually experienced. It is non-alcoholic but is recognised as having a slightly narcotic effect if drunk in sufficient quantity. When taken socially it follows a much more relaxed protocol. People come and go and each round is usually spaced by doleful songs, sung to the accompaniment of guitars. Such a session may last several hours at the end of which time the participants will be seen to stagger away and the Fijians will say they are "drunk" though they are careful to distinguish between those drunk with alcohol and those under the influence of "grog" which is how *yaqona* is referred to colloquially.

KAVA CEREMONY AT WAYA ISL: VISITED WITH MOSESE & MET WIFE & CHILDREN.

MAKING AND BLESSING THE KAVA

Meke, the call rings across the village common and the chorus, with the accompaniment of the *lali* (wooden drum) begins a chant. The chorus sits in a tightly packed circle and as the introduction ends, begins another verse. At this point a line of dancers emerges. It may be a group of women as in the picture above. But it could be men performing any of a number of dances. The most favoured are former war challenges: club and spear *mekes*. The dances are still performed on important occasions and also as entertainment commissioned by the Blue Lagoon Cruises for its guests. In each case the performers strive for the points we all find most admirable: attractive costumes, graceful movements with precision timing; energy and vigour where it is called for and style. Above all, style especially when it comes to humour.

Above, women performing at Yasawa i Rara. *Opposite*, the *meke* group from the village of Naisisili entertaining on board.

There are only two islands in the Yasawa group which were alienated to outside ownership during the past century. These are Tavewa, and Nanuya Levu now known as Turtle Island. Part of the island of Nanuya Lailai was also purchased from its Fijian owners and 50 acres of this island is owned by the Blue Lagoon Cruises company.

Tavewa Island is owned by the descendants of the Irishman, William Doughty. He purchased the island from a German planter, Frederick Hennings who grew cotton there in the 1860s. Doughty married the chief's daughter from Nacula and they had six children, among them Jack and Lucy Doughty, featured here. William's first wife died and he remarried, taking a part-European woman as his wife and had a further six children, and when she died, he married again, this time with a European woman. They had no children. William turned the island into a copra plantation and used to take his produce to Levuka in sailing schooners which were built on the island. In all he had six boats as each was lost to hurricanes. Jack's father Harry came from the first marriage. His mother was the daughter of the chief at Nacula. He went to the mainland to seek work, leaving Jack to look after his grandfather who died in 1926.

Jack spent more than twenty years on the mainland after his grandfather died and in 1952 returned to the island to cut copra and live off the land.

He is more than 70 years old now, but still active. He lives in a wooden cottage, which he built more than 30 years ago and enjoys visitors. Jack never married and lives alone.

Left, Jack poses in the "lounge" of his house. Though it looks flimsy, the house has survived many hurricanes. The beach outside his door is magnificent with a sweeping view to Matacawalevu. The house is tucked away among coconut palms and hibiscus and frangipani shrubs.

Lucy Doughty was a teacher and has retired to the island and lives with her son, daughter-in-law and grandchild.

Left, an aerial view of Turtle Island taken from the south. A small part of Tavewa Island may be seen on the left and Nacula to the north. The peak of Sawa i Lau may be seen in the far distance. Turtle Island was purchased more than ten years ago by an eccentric American, Richard Evanson. Richard's aim at that time, he says, was to find and secure a remote retreat which would take him away from Western civilisation and the problems it had caused him — a broken marriage and an addiction to alcohol. In buying Turtle Island, Richard found himself. The hard work of clearing scrub, building a house, putting in a jetty and organising his days into minutes, gave him the purpose to save himself. Richard gave up alcohol completely and with dedication turned Turtle Island into an exclusive resort where a limited number of guests can indulge their fantasies as the couple (above) is doing — having a champagne picnic with crab and lobster as the main course.

As the aerial photo shows, Turtle Island is spectacular with a fringe of turquoise reefs giving way to white sand beaches. The island is approximately 600 acres in extent and has twelve beaches — one for each couple. Richard has limited the number of guests to 24 at any given time. The beauty of the island was acknowledged by Hollywood twice when the movie, *The Blue Lagoon*, was shot with the island as the location. It was first shot in 1948 with Jean Simmons and Lloyd Bridges in the title roles and again in 1979 with Brooke Shields and Chris Atkins.

Those of us who have known Richard Evanson over the past 12 years cannot believe the change in him. From an overweight indulger he has turned into a trim, dedicated marathoner whose energy pours out in an overpowering flow. Joe Naisali was 17 years old when he signed on to work for Richard in 1972. That was the year of hurricane Bebe. Imagine a 17-year-old village boy arriving to join Richard and being greeted by a tent, where Richard slept, a shed where he kept all his crates of beer and spirits, an electric generator which chugged away happily to power a refrigerator which stood in solitary splendour among the coconut trees and whose contents were exclusively cans of beer! Richard and Joe survived the hurricane which took away their tent, demolished the shed and generally caused havoc, blowing over a huge bunyan tree which provided the shelter for the two men. They crawled in amongst the roots and waited for the storm to pass.

Richard is a compulsive man. No one would have believed that an alcoholic who would go to the lengths he did to drink would ever be able to give it up. That he

did must be due to his new compulsion — a dedicated mission to turn his island into a South Sea paradise of exotic birds, flowering trees and shrubs and flowers and a garden of lush tropical fruits. If he has his way, Turtle Island will become as close as it is possible to a garden of Eden.

Richard was born to working class parents on the West Coast of the United States. He was a bright child and won a place at Harvard University where he graduated with honour in business administration. He returned to the West Coast, married the daughter of a prominent family and went to work to make his first million. He chose cable television and made several million dollars. But after his marriage ended in divorce he sought to escape in the South Pacific.

Fiji was about as far as he could go from the West Coast. Its friendliness and charm was infectious. Richard applied for residence and then purchased Turtle Island with a view to retreating from the world.

Above, Richard Evanson with his horse on the beach in front of Turtle Island Lodge.

Above, A view from the top of Turtle Island at sunset looking north. The island in the far distance is Tavewa, home of the Doughtys. Nanuya Lailai is in the middle distance and Matacawalevu just visible on the left.

Richard Evanson fascinates all who know him. He has an overpowering personality and you either like him or are put off. But whether you like him as all his guests do, or are turned off, you still cannot deny the scope of his personal achievement. He has quit booze, got himself into shape and built the most exclusive resort in Fiji. In the process he has created a cash-flow which is allowing him to turn the island into a tropical paradise. Now that he has found himself, he wants others to share his dream Island. With missionary zeal he seeks to satisfy those fantasies that people dream of finding on a tropical island paradise: very friendly staff and guests, first-rate secluded accommodation, lobster, crab, fresh quail eggs, lagoon fish, prime steak and everything is inclusive in the tariff: champagne by the magnum for breakfast, luncheon and dinner. Wines, spirits and ales, crab or lobster omelette for breakfast; barbecues, exclusive picnics on any one of the 12 beaches with a fresh luncheon delivered by paddlecanoe; there are snorkelling trips, windsurfing, deep sea fishing, horse-riding, hiking, and trips to nearby villages.

Richard sought a wilderness to escape modern civilisation, but in Fiji, on the nearby islands, he has found an old civilisation from which the nicest, warmest and friendliest people on earth emerge. Therefore, for himself and for the sake of his lovely staff he asks that only nice, down-to-earth, friendly, fun loving, sociable people visit his island.

Opposite, top, the fishermen bring in the catch for the Turtle Island lunch. The Yasawa Islands abound with reef fish, lobster and crab and Turtle has contracted fishermen to supply its daily needs. Because there are not more than 24 guests (12 couples) at any one time, this is not difficult. Stranded, guests from Turtle Island push their boat into the water after being left high and dry by the tide. *Above,* Manager, Martin Livington on H.M.S. *Turtle,* with guests, staff and crew on the way to an excursion.

In reflecting on Richard Evanson and his island, I have come to the conclusion that he has been exceptionally clever. He has created a fantasy which can never be resolved. For as long as he lives there will be positive decisions to make. At present he is creating a park near the reception area, and when this is finished work will begin on a vast freshwater reservoir and when the reservoir is full, the water will be ducted to the gardens and trees he is planting around the island. His imagination leaps to aquaculture of black pearls; prawns and there is such a rush of words, that your head spins. There will be no empty old age for Richard.

Above, Long Beach is on the opposite side of the island. It is a crescent of powdery white sand which curves away for nearly a half-mile on the edge of translucent water. Horse riding is an inclusive recreation option on the island.

Left, the beach at Turtle Island Lodge with one of the accommodation *bures* just visible among the greenery. It was in fact the *bure* used by Brooke Shields during the filming of *The Blue Lagoon.*

It would be difficult to find a picture more appropriate for this book's title: *Blue Lagoons and Beaches*. Yes, the colour is real as those who have been to the Yasawa Islands will confirm. The view shows Turtle Island's Dolphin Beach.

Most days a Turtle Airways float plane swoops into the bay to either set down or pick up guests for the lodge. It is an occasion for guests and staff to walk down the length of the jetty to see the arrivals, but more specially to say farewell to new friends. It is usually a remarkable scene — not so much because of the singing and dancing but for the tears. If I had a dollar for every tear that has fallen on the jetty over the past few years, I could probably make Richard an offer for his island.

Richard established Turtle Airways to service his island, but the company is now owned by South Sea Cruises and its fleet of float planes take passengers wherever they wish to go around Fiji, but specially to the Yasawa Islands and to the Mamanuca group.

A series of coral limestone upthrusts are to be found throughout the Yasawa Islands and none are more spectacular than the 300 metre (1000 ft) peak of Sawa i Lau. Less well-known, but equally impressive is the upthrust at the south-western tip of Yaqeta Island. The porous limestone has created a series of caves including one large cave near the summit of the upthrust 300 metres above the beach. It was here that the people would retreat in times of war and await its resolution. Alipate, seen above on the right, with our guide Ratu Joe, centre and Lepane on the left, had been shown the cave some years ago and though he knew its general location, led us by a circuitous route to its entrance. Even here, hierarchical status was maintained: the chief had his own annex and there was another smaller cave for women about to give birth. The chief's cave is now the domain of the tiny and rare Fijian bat which we disturbed in large numbers and then photographed.

Right, a view from the top of the cave towards the north of Yaqeta Island. The high peak, top left, is the southern tip of Matacawalevu and to its right, Turtle Island.

The huge upthrust of coral limestone which is the island of Sawa i Lau is honeycombed with caves, including the most famous cave where visitors bathe. A number of other caves lead off from the principal one. These are accessible to the bold, who must dive under the overhanging rock and emerge on the other side. As you are diving into darkness, such an act requires considerable courage. The question foremost in your mind is the one I asked myself: will I be able to hold my breath long enough to get through? In former times (when I first dived the cave) sturdy Fijian crew from the boat would guide the visitor. As you dived to go under the overhang you would get a good shove and the man on the inside, looking out into the light of the main cave, would see you coming and grab you and pull you up. Recently I dived the cave with scuba equipment and discovered that there were caves, within caves and still more caves. An Australian doctor, Bob Richardson, went in with me, but decided to explore and when he was three caves in, suddenly lost his sense of direction and later admitted to having experienced considerable excitement. The logical thing would have been to have paid out a line to come back on. Bob found his way out, but some time ago an islander from Naviti disappeared. His body was never found.

ASAELI VATHINI TAWAKE

"ASAELI" AT HOME AT (YASAWA I RARA)
WITH BROTHER & FATHER

1985

80

The people of the Yasawa Islands acknowledge their traditional chiefs and give them the respect which custom demands. There are greater chiefs and lesser chiefs according to the sway their families had in former times. Each village in the island group has a chief and each island usually also acknowledges a paramount family.

Opposite, the Tui Yasawa from the village of Yasawa i Rara poses with his sons in his house.

The chief of Vuaki Village, Matacawalevu Island, suffers from an enlarged goitre. Guests at Turtle Island have so far subscribed more than $1500 towards the cost of sending the chief for an operation in New Zealand. *Above right,* the chief of Navotua Village, Nacula Island.

In former times chiefs had the power of life and death over their subjects, but even so, a chief's power depended on the strength of those who would follow him or on his ability to coerce support. In the Yasawa Islands no one chief was able to subjugate the others and thus form a political confederation as happened in eastern Fiji. Because they were unable to unite, the people of the group were vulnerable to invading parties from the mainland.

Since cession of Fiji to Britain in 1874, war was abolished and in the intervening period up to independence in 1970, the people of the Yasawas have intermarried so that today they resemble a large family.

Fijians have an incredibly close sense of family. In former times kinship groups with a wide network of relatives were much more likely to survive. If one branch of an extensive family was beaten in war it could fall back on customary hospitality of another. The bigger the group, the more men it could muster and the greater its power. Even though such groups generally presented a united front against a common enemy, the way was always open to intrigue. The powerful Rewan state of Bure-basaga fell to Bau because of rivalry between the sons of the paramount chief; one branch joining Bau and falling on their unsuspecting relatives.

The practical advantage of a network of relatives today is the support it offers an individual away from home. When I motored round the Yasawa Island in a small boat with Ratu Joe he said there would be no need for tents and cooking utensils as he had relatives in *every* village and we could be sure of being looked after. All we needed was *yaqona* and food which we would share with the families we stayed with. There was never any question of seeking accommodation. No sooner was our boat in sight and Joe identified and the word would pass through the village so that by the time we were on the beach one of his cousins, or uncles or aunties would be waiting for us.

Our host at the village of Soso, Naviti, was Joe Seremia, a 28-year-old cousin of Ratu Joe, and his wife Vaciseva. Joe had spent two years cruising the Pacific with an Australian yacht but gave up thoughts of settling in Australia when on a visit home he fell in love and married.

The people of central and southern Yasawa Islands send children to high school to the island of Naviti. As well as schoolwork, children take part in the normal daily routine of planting and fishing. This is both a part of their education and an important supplement to their diet. The photo above was taken at the start of the mid-year term. Gangs of pupils, armed with the all purpose "bush knives" were detailed to "mow" the grass around the school compound. You will seldom see a Fijian without his knife as it has so many uses.

Above, three future "femme fatale" regard the camera at the Yasawa Centenary Memorial Junior and Secondary School, Naviti. *Right*, their teacher, Noa Ravu, supervises a work group. He says the children do well in any comparison with pupils on the mainland and ascribes this to a settled, supportive environment.

PREPARING THE LOVO FOR A FEAST.

THE PIG IS CLEANED & WRAPPED IN COCONUT FROND - TO PUT IN THE LOVO.

Fijian life is still subject to a number of customary rituals. Among these are mortuary rituals. The death, burial and mourning periods are divided by social gatherings involving the presentation of tabua, the serving of *yaqona*, presentation of fine mats and the presentation and cooking of food which is later divided and shared. *Opposite*, the *lovo* (earth oven) pit where stones have been heating is cleared of unburnt pieces of wood and embers which would otherwise burn the food. *Opposite below*, a pig is deftly parcelled in a coconut frond in preparation for the oven. *Right*, the presentation of food. *Below*, the placement of the food in the *lovo*.

Sometimes, as I wandered among villages, I had the feeling that I was part of a giant campout. These two views suggest a calm and easy pace but also a charm which is most appealing.

The views here are part of the ceremony of *vakabogi tini* performed ten days after a funeral at the village of *Yaqeta, Yaqeta Island*. The scene looks romantically attractive but think of it on a rainy day. Firewood is the universal fuel in the Yasawa Islands and the art of cooking consists mainly of the *lovo* and the boiling pot. This may suggest simple bland food and for the most part that is what it is, though, as I discovered, it can also be intricate and deliciously different. Once in the interior I had wild pork chopped fine and cooked with pumpkin and chili; a Rewan specialty is to serve prawns with coconut cream, onion and young *dalo* leaves cooked in the *lovo* and there are many ways of serving shellfish, fish, seaweed, vegetables, fruits and such exotic delicacies as tender fern shoots.

The Fijians are physical people as befits their warrior past. The only form of power on most of the islands is manpower, except where horses are kept. From an early age children are trained to fetch and carry. *Opposite*, Fijians love rugby and outstanding players are universally admired. It is an opportunity to display strength, speed, balance and grace as well as courage — qualities which are the hallmark of an attractive man.

Vitality and vigour are the natural attributes of health and well-being. The overall impression in the Yasawa Islands is one of peace and quiet. The trade wind blows through the coconut palms, the surf booms on the far reef and little seems to happen. But occasionally the visitor is caught up in a burst of activity. No sooner does it seem to have begun and it seems to end. Children rush into the water for a noonday break from class, a horse gallops past on the beach or a punt with an outboard engine echoes across the water and then is heard no more.

In the Yasawa Islands the sea is a fact of life. You cannot go anywhere unless you cross it. It is a barrier to those who may want to go and to those who may want to visit. But it is also a storehouse of food. Both men and women are taught early how to exploit the resources of the reef, lagoon and ocean. Young girls accompany their mothers and aunties and young boys, their fathers and uncles. The women seek out shellfish, octopus, seaslugs, crabs, edible seaweeds and such fish as they can conveniently catch in tidal pools and with a handline. The men set nets, conduct fishdrives, dive for spearfishing, use handlines in deep water and go out at night.

Yasawa Islanders are good sailors. They enjoy the sea. Visitors cannot fail but be amazed at their first sighting of a small canoe made from roofing iron! These are highly unstable and easily swamped and yet they are used with confidence even in rough weather. I tried one and found it difficult to control. Wooden, flat bottom punts are more commonly used to move about from island to island. These are usually powered by an outboard engine. The fisherman (above) was successfully hand-lining near a drop-off on the edge of a coral reef. He had set up his fishing bag and fishing line on a tripod made from driftwood to make his effort more comfortable. At certain times of the year small sardine-like fish known locally as *daniva* swarms near the shore. An expert with a throwing net can quickly get a sackful. The fish is regarded as a delicacy and it is also used as bait.

LOBSTERS, LOBSTERS, & MORE LOBSTERS! BUT GOOD.

One of my most exciting experiences was a night out with lobster fishermen from Somosomo Village, Naviti Island. They came to fish off Matacawalevu and by necessity it had to be a moonless night. The three fishermen — seen above displaying some of their catch — spent more than two hours in the cold dark water and got more than 70 lobster and some crabs. I was considerably better off in my thick neoprene wetsuit which kept me warm and snug from coral scratches. Each fisherman carried an underwater flashlight and a rubber sling with the aid of which he fired a mild steel rod. The fishing was conducted in water between four metres and one metre in depth. When fishing in the shallows we were subject to a surf surge. A wave would pick you up, carry you a metre or two and then the backwash would sweep you back again. It was marvellous to see how deftly my companions could fire their slings as they were being swept past the lobster and how expertly they would pick up both on the return sweep. A young boy followed in the punt. After more than two hours in the water, the fishermen who were by now almost frozen, called a halt.

Right, a favourite Fijian way to catch fish — stalking the tidal flats with a throwing spear.

The mangrove areas of the Yasawa Islands play an important environmental role. What the sea takes away, the mangroves try to reclaim elsewhere. A mangrove forest, with its tangle of aerial roots, is a forebidding place at low water. It is a fertile ground for a great deal of marine life. The tangle of roots and trunks provides shelter for juvenile fish and the mud is honeycombed with crabs and shellfish, including the delicious *qari* (mud crab) being demonstrated opposite. The crabs were caught by the girl's mother in the mangroves immediately behind her.

In times of war, women and children were sometimes hidden in a mangrove forest.

During my time in the Yasawa Islands I spent more than ten hours underwater with scuba equipment and several hours more with a snorkel. The islands enjoy excpetionally clear water. This is due to the fact that they are a long way from the mainland and out of reach of the silt and sediment carried into the sea by large rivers and because little rain falls in the Yasawas and therefore there is little run-off. Because of the great number of reefs, marine life is prolific. It is a spectacular wonderland but that is not how the Fijians see it. To them it is a vast storehouse of food which you tap according to need or according to taste.

Above, Ratu Joe with a parrot fish which he has shot with his sling. *Opposite*, fish caught by my camera.

The rock cod featured above has the unusual name of "Fat Albert". I am not sure how it got its name. It lives just off the jetty at Turtle Island where it appears each morning and waits to be fed. There are several other cod; a number of squirrel fish, trevally, sardines, mullet and banded perch amongst others. It is a good place for a photographer.

The pictures on these two pages were taken at the cabbage coral patch which lies in the sheltered water between Tavewa, Matacawalevu, Nanuya Lailai and Nacula. It is a huge coral, rising some 15 metres to near the surface and spreading out more than 10 metres in diameter. Beautiful soft corals, whips and corgonians hang on its underside and the area teems with fish.

The iguana shown above is a native of Fiji and a cousin to its much more rare banded iguana, found only in Fiji. It is a shy creature which lives in the bush and is seldom seen. The specimen above is one of several kept in an enclosure at Turtle Island for the benefit of visitors.

The people of the Yasawa Islands own and operate a variety of boats and among these are shoal-draft cutters which regularly make passage to Lautoka. They carry copra, goats, artefacts and people and return with rice, flour, sugar, tea, kerosene, petrol and diesel among other things. The boats are owned by family or partnership groups and sometimes, as in the case above, by villages. This one is owned co-operatively by the village of Soso, Naviti.

The art of construction of traditional houses is very much alive and well in Fiji, but particularly in the Yasawa Islands. As in the past, the materials are gathered locally and assembled. The person for whom the house is to be built, co-opts relatives and friends so that the task can be accomplished quickly. Construction begins with the placement of the four principal uprights and the main frame. This is generally lashed into place, but for those who can afford it, nails are quicker. The outer frame is covered by scantlings and braces and then the inner covering is put into place. As this stage is completed, teams of men emerge from the bush with bundles of thatching grass which is lashed into place. Long pieces of split bamboo are usually preferred for the sides and these are lashed into place with bark. The final stage is the capping of the ridgepole and in the photo above, two men prepare the rope for the capping. This is done ingeniously by twisting a strip of bark over a tough but pliable jungle creeper.

The larger the number of workers, the quicker the task completed. Though the labour is contributed without payment in cash, there are customary obligations: the house owner feeds his workers once each day and in the future — if he has not done so in the past — will contribute his labour to them. *Opposite top*, the *bure* almost completed with the ridgepole and capping thatch being lashed into place. *Opposite*, the customary afternoon meal for the builders. *Above*, a good example of a well-made *bure*.

In departing from the *bure* Fijians have not yet settled on any one style.

But even among *bure* there can be obvious differences. There are imposing *bure* for chiefs and lesser ones for others.

Regardless of the exterior or whether the house is a *bure* or one built with modern materials, the interior has a distinct Fijian style. The house (above) is occupied by Jone Toe and his family. He is a teacher at the Naviti school and invited me home for tea during the mid-morning break.

This view is of the interior of the chief's *bure* at Naisisili Village, Nacula Island. It is acknowledged as one of the finest examples of its type in the Yasawa Islands.

The economy of the Yasawa Islands is mostly subsistence with the necessities for daily life won from the lagoon and the bush. The principal occupation of the men is planting and fishing while women concern themselves with domestic duties and child care. While they are clearly defined, male and female roles overlap. Women are sometimes active in the bush and men will sometimes cook.

Clearing and planting is definitely a masculine chore and invariably it is more pleasant when done in company as seen in the photo top left. The grass and scrub has been cleared for a cassava plantation.

I believe it has happened, but I have yet to see a woman climb a coconut tree. *Above*, a plantation high up a slope above the village of Soso on Naviti Island, displays a healthy crop of cassava and pineapple. Our guide and host at Somosomo, Naviti, Seveci Naisele, about to take a pineapple from his plantation for a mid-morning snack. Seveci who neither drinks *yaqona* nor alcohol nor smokes cigarettes because of religious beliefs, is recognised as an outstanding planter and fisherman. He says that since he turned to a righteous life, his energy has increased ten-fold. The only problem with his increased production is that it has attracted those who are less industrious who come to "borrow".

While they obtain the immediate necessities of life from the land and sea as they have done for the past millenium. Yasawa Islanders say they are cash poor and increasingly they need more to buy the extras they have become used to: tea, sugar, rice, flour, tobacco, clothes, cement, glass, tools, roofing iron, outboard and diesel engines and their fuel, kerosene, soap and detergent, canned meat, fishing lines and hooks and school fees amongst other things. The price of copra (left) is now beginning to pick up but on its own, it cannot hope to meet growing aspirations. Some villages have formed fishing co-operatives with spectacular results; others have gone into goat farming. Women collect shells and make artefacts for the tourist trade whilst wages paid to the crew of the Blue Lagoon boats go almost exclusively to men from the Yasawas as it also does on Turtle Island. There is a growing acceptance that tourism will play a greater role in the economy of the islands in the future.

Since the advent of Christianity which radically altered the way of life in the Yasawas one hundred years ago, change has come slowly. I am sure this has been a good thing as rapid change has a destabilising effect on small, rural communities. The people here live their life according to their ancient customs and rituals. These customs and rituals have sustained them for countless generations, keeping their communities functional. There is always something to think about, some obligation to render to chief, relative or neighbour; some festival to attend, some contribution to make, a sporting event to take part in or a voyage to visit distant relatives and friends. To an outsider village life seems confined and monotonous. To the villager it can be as crowded as he likes to make it. Visitors are prone to be either swept away by the romance of what they see as an idyllic way of life or to concede that "it's nice for them, but I could not live like that." But most miss the real point. This is to recognise the freedom of the Yasawa Islander to live as he or she pleases.

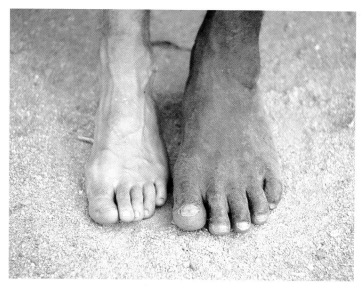

My foot and his foot.

Ratu Joe

Last page, last word:

The title of this book could easily have been *Footloose in the Yasawas* or perhaps *Barefoot in the Blue Lagoon* if only my feet were like Ratu Joe's!

But the purpose of this last page is to say thank you to all those who have made this volume possible. Foremost amongst these are the people of the Yasawa Islands who welcomed me to their shores and put up with my invasion of their privacy. I owe a great debt to Blue Lagoon Cruises and the support of David Wilson and Andrew Drysdale. Richard Evanson of Turtle Island deserves special thanks for his enthusiastic support of my project — he fed me, gave me accommodation, provided a boat and Ratu Joe as my guide so that I could visit all the islands in the group. I also used his scuba equipment and even his underwater camera which was a new model and superior to my own. The idea for the project received enthusiastic support from the General Manager of the Fiji Visitors Bureau, Malakai Gucake, without whose help it would not have been possible. I hope I have done justice to their expectations.

My friend Ratu Joe deserves special mention. Even though he worked on the set of the movie, *The Blue Lagoon*, and played a role as one of the extras, he found it hard to cope with my enthusiasm, especially when it came to climbing most of the peaks of the group so I could get my pictures. But he came along, carried some of the equipment and tried his best to be enthusiastic in a task which to his way of thinking must have seemed bizarre.

Every photographer suffers anxiety until he has seen his film processed and confirmed that everything is as it should be. My good friend Ikbal Jannif, of Caines Photofast, Suva, arranged priority to be given to the processing of the film chosen for the assignment: the new Kodak Ektachrome EN 100 colour reversal stock. The pictures were shot with 35 mm cameras and then dispatched from Turtle Island by Turtle Airways to Nadi from where they were delivered to the Caines Photofast's Nadi Depot, sent overnight to Suva, processed and returned to Nadi the following night so that I would have them within three days of dispatch. I must compliment Ikbal and his laboratory staff for the excellence of their work and the speed with which they accomplished it. The new emulsion at a rating of 100 ISO is faster than my old favourite, Ektachrome ER 64. This is a help in low-light situations. It is also more neutral, in my view, having lost some of the blueness for which the ER emulsion was often criticised. Those who are interested in technical details can judge the results for themselves: the plates shown here are a good representation of the photos I shot. It should be noted, however, that the printing of plates in a book is the result of an entirely different process to that of producing photo prints. Photoprints are the result of the transference of the negative or positive image onto a specially coated light-sensitive emulsion. When the image has been transferred, it is then "developed" with various chemical processes. To produce plates for a book, the process involves the "scanning" of a negative or transparency so that the four primary colours are separated. Plates made for each colour are inked appropriately and the image transferred to sheets of paper. It may well be that much more could have been made from the transparencies chosen for this book if they were produced by an expert as photo prints.

This has been one of the most enjoyable assignments I have been involved with over the past 25 years. I hope my pleasure in the task is reflected for others to see.

James Siers, 1985

AT BEAUTIFUL CASTAWAY ISLAND & ON THE YASAWA PRINCESS EVERYONE LOVED ROGER AND CALLED HIM RATU ROGER & MAI MAI IRENE xx MARAMA.

"NI SA BULA"

A FIJI EXPERIENCE IS THE MOST BEAUTIFUL THING THAT ANYONE COULD WISH FOR. THE PEOPLE ARE SO GRACIOUS, KIND, FRIENDLY, HAPPY & STILL UNSPOILED. I HOPE & PRAY THAT WE SHALL NOT DESTROY ANY OF THIS BEAUTY, AND NATURAL LIFE STYLE FOR MANY YEARS TO COME.

OH YES, THEY NEED TOURISM TO HELP WITH SOME OF THEIR MODERN NEEDS. WE HAVE RECOGNISED SOME CHANGES DURING THE PAST 5 YEARS, WITH THE INFLUX OF NEW ZEALAND & AUSTRALIAN INVESTORS; BUT LET US NOT RUIN THESE BEAUTIFUL PEOPLE & THEIR GLORIOUS HABITAT.

I WONDER WHY WE CANT VISIT, ENJOY, LAUGH SING & PLAY WITH THEM & BE SO GRATEFUL TO ENJOY THESE PLEASURES, WITHOUT WANTING TO TAKE OVER — CHANGE THEIR LIFE STYLE TO OURS WHICH LEAVES MUCH TO BE DESIRED AS WE ALL VERY WELL KNOW.

FIJI IS STILL BEAUTIFUL AND UNSPOILED, BUT I KNOW YOU HAVE A DIFFICULT TIME TO KEEP IT THIS WAY, ESPECIALLY WITH THE INDIAN POPULATION CONTROLLING ALL THE BUSINESS! I CAN ONLY HOPE THAT YOU WILL STAY AS LOVELY AS YOU ARE, FOR SOME MORE YEARS.

"SA MOCE" FROM ROGER — RATU ROGER
IRENE — MARAMA IRENE.

VINAKA VAKU LEVU

FOR YOUR FRIENDSHIP & KINDNESS.

ISA LEI, NA NOQU RARAWA
NI KO SA NA VODO E NA MATAKA
BAU NANUMA, NA NODATOU LASA
MAI NANUYA NANUMA TIGOGA

ISA LEI, THE PURPLE SHADOWS FALL
SAD THE MORROW WILL DAWN UPON MY SORROW
OH FORGET NOT WHEN YOU ARE FAR AWAY
PRECIOUS MOMENTS BESIDE NANUYA BAY.

O'ER THE OCEAN YOUR ISLAND HOME IS CALLING
HAPPY COUNTRY WHERE ROSES BLOOM IN SPLENDOUR
IF I COULD BUT JOURNEY THERE BESIDE YOU
THEN FOREVER MY HEART WOULD SING IN RAPTURE.

"ISA LEI."